REPORT WRITING
IN BUSINESS

REPORT WRITING IN BUSINESS

Trevor J. Bentley

**Kogan
Page**

published by Kogan Page Ltd
in association with
The Chartered Institute of Management Accountants

Incorporated by Royal Charter
63 PORTLAND PLACE, LONDON W1N 4AB

First published 1978 by The Chartered
Institute of Management Accountants
Reprinted 1980, 1983, 1985

Copyright © ICMA 1978

This indexed edition published in Great Britain in 1987
by Kogan Page Ltd
120 Pentonville Road, London N1 9JN

Reprinted 1988, 1990, 1992

British Library Cataloguing in Publication Data
Bentley, Trevor J.
    Report writing in business.—
    2nd ed.
    1. Business report writing
    I. Title
    808'.066658   HF5719

    ISBN 1-85091-325-8

Printed and bound in Great Britain by
Biddles Ltd, Guildford and King's Lynn

CONTENTS

Foreword   7

Chapter

1 — Introduction   9

2 — Objectives   12

3 — Approach   14

4 — Content   24

5 — Form   28

6 — Numbering   30

7 — Production   32

8 — Distribution and follow up   37

9 — Conclusion   39

Further Reading List   40

Examples

Example I   — Persuasive Report   42

        II   — Explanatory Report   49

        III   — Discussive Report   59

        IV   — Informative Report   70

Index   85

FOREWORD

I am very pleased to see the publication by our Institute of a book on the vital topic of report writing in business.

Many candidates at our examinations perform inadequately, not because of a lack of knowledge of their subject, but because of their inability to answer the questions in an effective manner. To these students this book now brings clear guidelines showing how written communications can be improved. I am sure that if the procedures explained in the book are consistently applied in the examination room candidates will achieve better results.

The lack of training in report writing also shows up in business life and prevents some members from being as effective as their technical skill would justify. To them and also to the more expert amongst us, Mr Bentley gives clear guidance on how to write every type of business report. He shows how to ensure that the report meets its aim and communicates a clear message to all recipients. Additionally there is valuable advice on the format of reports and the methods of production. To complete the work there is a varied selection of specimen reports.

I am sure that in meeting these many needs this book will provide a valuable addition to our publications. It should have a wide appeal to both students and members and to all others eager to get their written message across clearly and competently.

L W RICE BSc(Econ) FCMA JDipMA ACIS
Chairman
Research and Technical Committee.

Chapter 1

INTRODUCTION

Written reports are perhaps the most frequently used method of presenting information to management. Reports are written by most accountants and managers and cover a wide range of topics from general reports on performance to reports on specific events.

Whatever the subject and purpose of the report, its preparation will call for an ability, which unfortunately is not widespread. Reports are a means of setting down the facts, opinions and conclusions which the author wishes to communicate. They are, or should be a vehicle for effective communication.

This booklet has been written to provide the reader with a practical guide to report writing in business. Communicating in writing demands a certain basic knowledge. This knowledge deals with:

- knowing what your aims are,
- knowing who your audience is and how you wish to approach it,
- knowing what you want to communicate,
- knowing how to do it.

Objective
The aim of the communication should be clear. Is it to pass on information, to persuade someone to take a particular course of action, to answer a question, to ask a question, to give instructions or simply to give pleasure? The objective is crucial for this affects the content and the format.

Every piece of writing should have a purpose. It is effective only if it achieves that purpose. It will not achieve the purpose if the reader does not read it. There is no way you can make someone read what you have written. He must, therefore, be encouraged at least to pick it up and start. From then on it's up to you.

Readability is the key to successful writing. People must find it easy to read and interesting. Readability can be achieved if the following simple rules are used:

(a) Ensure you start on a high point of interest. The title must catch the reader's attention much the same as a headline does in a newspaper.

(b) Other points of interest must be introduced approximately every 500 words. This will of course depend upon the text but in report writing 500 words gives plenty of time for the previous point to sink in.

(c) Avoid using mathematical formulae or detailed statistical tables in the main body of the report.

(d) Finish on a high point which almost leaves the reader breathless.

The need to consider the reader's interest is vital if you wish to put your message over.

The Audience

The audience you are trying to reach via your writing will affect the language you use, the length of the piece, the format of the work and the style. Jargon should be avoided at all costs. Jargon is the unnecessary use of technical terms. It is as refreshing to read jargon free writing as it is to hear jargon free speech.

Your audience may be trained in receiving, reading and understanding reports, on the other hand they may not. The method of presentation should allow for this difference in ability. The reader should not be expected to climb up to your literary level. He won't so don't attempt to make him.

Keep the language simple. Check you have done this by calculating the Fogg index. This is done by adding the words in each sentence and calculating the average sentence length. To this is added the percentage of words in the piece that have more than two syllables. A good readable level is 30, below this it is difficult to maintain flow and interest. Above 30 the work becomes increasingly difficult to read.

Deciding on the length of the written work is important. If it is too short you fail to get the message across; too long and you lose your reader. Finding a balance is not easy. One method that can be used is to write the piece then try to reduce every paragraph by at least one sentence. Good editing is important. With practice the editing becomes less a process of mutilation and more a process of amendment.

Choosing the most appropriate format depends again on who it is for. Some individuals like to receive correspondence and reports in a certain form. If so, use that form. If the choice is yours, think about the people concerned; the time they will have to read it, and how involved and interested they are.

Style comes with experience. Let it happen naturally. Attempting to develop a style will lead to an unnatural flow. Start by writing what you want, how you want, and take it from there.

Content

Many people feel that the content is a constraint on how they write. It should not affect how you write, only the form that you use. In later sections the handling of certain specific content is dealt with; for the moment it will suffice to say that you decide the content once the objective has been established. Written presentation in all its forms is a powerful communicative device if used properly. Unfortunately many people do not give it the attention it deserves and consequently many desks are piled high with unwanted, unreadable paperwork.

The Method

The aim of this booklet is to provide an insight into the methods of effective reporting writing. Knowing what you want to say, to whom and the reason, is of no avail if you cannot say it effectively.

Chapter 2
OBJECTIVES

Before setting pen to paper the report writer should ask himself

'Why am I writing this report?'

There are many apparent answers from

'Because I have been asked to' to 'I don't know'.

The only valid answer to the question must consist of a specific objective.

No report should be written without a clearly defined objective. There are four principal reasons for writing reports but each report regardless of the type will have it's own specific objective. If this is not clear to the writer then there is little if any hope of the report being effective.

The principal reasons for writing reports are:

— to obtain agreement to a course of action	— **Persuasive**
— to explain specific events	— **Explanatory**
— as a basis for discussion	— **Discussive**
— to inform	— **Informative.**

Persuasive Reports

Writing persuasive reports is not a simple process. It is necessary to write clearly and concisely and to present arguments in such a way that the reader fully understands the writer's thoughts and to ensure an understanding of the processes leading to his recommendations. The report writer cannot report all the data and information which he has collected throughout the work he has done. He must therefore be able to summarize the information in a form which allows for a full appreciation of the subject matter.

In obtaining agreement the author must write his report in a particular way that persuades the reader to accept his recommendations. This calls for a special approach and a structure which helps to achieve the objective.

Explanatory Reports

Many reports are written for the sole purpose of ex   ..g
certain events. These can vary from complex reports or major
disasters to simple reports on customer complaints. This type of
report calls for an approach which clearly sets out facts and can be
seen by the reader to be unbiased and fully explain the event under
review.

Discussive Reports

Discussions can be significantly improved if there is a written
basis for the discussion. Reports for discussion purposes are often
referred to as 'papers'. Regardless of the name given to the document they form a special type of report which requires a particular
approach.

Informative Reports

The transmission of information from one person to another is
achieved in a variety of ways, both verbal and written. Whichever
method is used it is only effective if it increases the listener's or
reader's knowledge. It must tell him something he did not already
know, or place an interpretation on known facts which he had not
considered. One of the commonest informative reports is the 'progress' report, the aim of which is to bring the reader up to date on
a specific subject.

The reason for writing the report will determine the methods
used. The objectives you wish to achieve will determine the exact
form and the content you use. Before starting work on a report the
writer should ask himself the following three questions in the order
given:

   (i)   'Why am I writing this report?'.
  (ii)   'Which type of report should it be?'
 (iii)   'What are the specific objectives I hope to achieve?'

Only when clear meaningful answers are available should the
report writing process begin.

Chapter 3

THE APPROACH

There are a number of rules which should be followed for all types of report. These are the basic rules of report writing. In addition each type of report has its own particular rules.

The basic rules follow:

Brevity
If you can say what you want to say in a dozen words do not write two hundred. Thin reports are attractive, easy to handle, cheap to produce, easy to change and usually much more readable. Nobody complains of the report being too short.

Simplicity
A report is a means of communication, it is not the place to prove your technical knowledge or your command of the English language. Only use words that everyone will be able to read and understand.

Purpose
Remember why you are writing the report and try to put yourself in your reader's shoes. It is all too easy to get lost in your writing. We all review our own writing as writers not as readers and consequently we often hide the message amongst too many words.

Begin
Have a meaningful beginning which explains the reason for the report and introduces the reader to the subject. If the reader is aware of the report and the subject he can always skip the beginning.

End
Always end by summarising how the report has achieved its objectives. You don't need to actually write 'the end' but the reader should be quite clear that he has reached the end.

Content
Make sure that the main content of the report is readable with points of interest well spaced throughout the report (e.g. every 500 words).

Jargon   Defined as 'the unnecessary use of technical terms,' should be vigorously avoided. If technical details are necessary keep them out of the body of the report.

Title   Give the report a meaningful name.

Author   Always name the writer or writers.

Date   Always date the report.

The basic rules should always be applied. If you consider them to be commonsense then we are part of the way to achieving the aims of this booklet. All too often these basic rules, whether commonsense or not, are ignored and the results can be found in the files of any organisation.

Perhaps one of the rules which is most overlooked by accountants concerns the use of jargon. Many people believe that words or abbreviations developed to cover technical expressions should be used to simplify reports. The definition of jargon states the 'unnecessary use of technical terms'. Choosing the time and place to use such technical expressions is difficult, the answer is to avoid them altogether. The following example taken from a real situation shows how this can be done.

'The important impact on DCF calculation of the latest Hyde proposals on CCA is concerned with relating net cashflow returns with the real returns consequent on valuing assets on a replacement basis'.

This sentence in context will be understood by accountants. If, however, the report was intended to inform management of the impact of inflation accounting, as in this case, then the following translation might have been more effective:

'The present procedures used for assessing new capital projects will be affected by the latest proposals on Inflation Accounting. The main area of impact will be relating the cash returns on the project with the returns calculated by increasing the original cost of capital to allow for inflation'.

The more specific rules applicable to individual reports depend on the type of report. Each of the four main types of report, persuasive, explanatory, discussive and informative have their own structure. It is within this framework that the specific rules apply.

Persuasive Reports (See Example I)

Reports written to obtain agreement should convince the reader of the validity of the arguments as the report proceeds. To do this it is vital to approach the report in a special way. The introduction should be followed immediately by a summary of the main recommendations. This method, referred to by many people as starting at the end, is used for a very practical reason. If the reader knows from the beginning what the conclusions are, he will read the report in a particular way. He will be looking for the facts and arguments that support the recommendations. If he is doing this then he is more likely to find them than if you leave him to read the report and develop his own conclusions.

The report is not a thriller, you are not trying to spring any surprises at the end. You are trying to convince the reader that a particular course of action should be followed. By concentrating his mind from the outset on this point you have a far greater chance of succeeding. To be effective this approach must be followed with care and understanding. It will take time and practice to become adept at writing this type of report. The guidelines given below should be an aid in organising the layout of a persuasive report!

- **Title page** — which will contain the date, the subject matter and the distribution of the report,
- **An introduction to the subject matter,**
- **A summary of recommendations,**
- **A summary of the present position,**
- **Scope of the survey,**
- **Observations on recommendations,**
- **Conclusion**
- **Appendices.**

Introduction

The introduction should detail the reason why the survey has been carried out, who asked for the survey to be done and the ultimate aim.

Summary of Recommendations

Each recommendation should be written briefly and clearly so that there is no doubt whatsoever about the suggestion being made. The recommendation should be short and simply state facts. The following are examples of concise recommendations:

1. that a visible record computer be introduced.
2. that the following systems are processed on the visible record computer:
   - Sales
   - Purchases
   - Accounts
   - Payroll
3. that the number of staff in the accounts department be reduced.
4. that the visible record computer be introduced within six months.
5. that the wages, cashiers, purchase, sales and invoicing departments be amalgamated.

The aim of summarizing recommendations is to enable the reader to obtain a ready grasp of the subject matter and be able to read the remainder of the report on the basis of justifying the recommendations.

Present Position

The report writer should write this as briefly as possible indicating the salient points and the problems which were found to exist at present. Putting this in the report enables the reader to focus on the reasons for the survey and the reasons for recommendations.

Scope of Survey

This is the section in which the report writer should describe clearly the work in the survey to enable the reader to see that the recommendations have been made after due consideration. Again, this should be a fairly brief section which should show what work has been done and the timetable followed.

Observation on Recommendations

In this section each recommendation and the reason for it is dealt with separately and fully, and a considerable amount of time should be spent on it. This section should form the basis of the arguments for and against each recommendation. The writer could do this by producing a balance sheet of 'pros' and 'con's' set out as below:

Pro's	Con's

Each observation should repeat the recommendation and, wherever possible, indicate that the recommendation has been arrived at with the agreement of those affected by its implications. This is perhaps the most important section of the report and provides the opportunity for the writer to present a clearly argued case for his recommendations.

Appendices

Appendices are extremely useful in removing detailed statistics, tables, volumes, etc., from the body of the report. If this is done, the body of the report will be much more readable, but there should be a cross-reference in the text to the relevant parts of the appendices. The need for appendices depends on the length and complexity of the report.

If the report is brief, then appendices will not be required, if it is complex then appendices can be used effectively.

If the reader finishes the report and is not in complete agreement, do not be surprised. What you are trying to achieve is basic agreement and an understanding of the content. There will always be a number of points that are queried. If the reader comments "Well on the whole I agree with your findings, but I have one or two questions" then you can be justly pleased with your efforts.

Explanatory Reports (See Example II)

Reports which set out to explain some event or situation, must be written in an unbiased way. They must be factual statements that do not lead the reader into arriving at a particular conclusion. For this reason they demand an approach almost the exact opposite to the persuasive report.

The twin enemies of the explanatory report are ambiguity and contradiction. These can largely be overcome by following the approach indicated below:

- title, author and date,
- introduction,
- persons/departments involved,
- sequence of events,
- action taken,
- cause and effect,
- conclusion.

Title

In this type of report it is important to state clearly the subject being explained. This is often done with a main title and a sub-title (see Example II).

Introduction

In this case the introduction should cover two main points:

- the reason for the report and who requested it;
- the position and authority of the author.

This should be done in such a way that the reader has a pen picture of the subject.

Persons Involved

A report of this nature is almost always about people. It is important, therefore, that if titles are used they are clear and unambiguous and if names are used it must be clear who the people are and the positions they hold.

Sequence of Events.

This is an historical analysis of the sequence of events from the beginning to the end of the subject being examined. No comment is made in this section on the specific actions or their causes. It should be a simple straight-forward record of what happened.

Action Taken

This section deals with every action, or the critical ones, in the same sequence as the historical analysis and sets out the reasons for the action. Where action was based on specific pieces of information these should be included as appendices. This section is the crux of the report.

Cause and Effect

Taking each act in sequence the results are analysed as to the cause and effect. This is the part of the report where the writer might find difficulty in remaining unbiased. It is very difficult not to add your own interpretation of causes and care must be taken to remain factual.

In most events which require explanation something is done at the end. This may correct problems or be disciplinary or even be an attempt to cover up the problem altogether. It is important to analyse these subsequent actions as these may change the readers view of the whole incident.

Conclusion

The final part of the report should state how the information has been gathered, how long it has taken and the accuracy of the content. Any missing evidence should be noted and comments made on its importance. The author should not draw his own conclusions or recommend action unless this has been specifically requested in the brief to prepare the report.

The important job of fact finding and marshalling content is dealt with in section four of the booket; it is a vital part of writing an explanatory report.

Discussive Reports (See Example III)

Discussion without a report has a marked disadvantage: it is lacking in purpose. It is not always possible in conversation to make the same logical and forceful points which can be placed in a report. The spoken word is of great value in emphasizing particular aspects, but statistics cannot be effectively considered nor can the full effect of a complex topic be appreciated only by listening. It has been said that two-thirds of what one hears is not registered by the brain.

Because of this, unless they are well-organized, discussions may fail to achieve their purpose. You may recall the old adage

"I hear   —   I forget

I see   —   I remember

I do   —   I understand".

To aid the discussion the report should not be written specifically to persuade or purely to explain. It is a mainly factual document but must allow sufficient latitude for discussion. Like the other types of report the discussive report has an aim to achieve. To do this it must be properly organized. The approach which experience has proved effective is as follows:

- title, author and date,
- introduction,
- scope and subject,
- discussion points,
- possible action,
- conclusion.

Introduction

This should state clearly that the report has been written as a basis for discussion and indicate the subject to be discussed. It is often useful to include here a note on how the report came to be written, who asked for it and why.

Scope of the Subject

It is important for the reader to be able to identify quite clearly what the subject is and the boundaries to the discussion. This section must set the scene for the discussion and should enable the chairman of the meeting to control the discussion within the boundaries indicated. The source of the content should be set down together with a note of the methods used to collect the information.

Discussion Points

Written in a number of ways, this section sets out the main points for discussion. It is helpful to the reader if each point is made and then the reason for discussing it given. Sufficient information must be provided for the reader to be able to comment on it in the discussion. People can and very often do stall action through lack of information; comments such as 'I need more information before I can comment' are heard regularly. The report writer should make sure that this is not the reaction to his report.

Possible Action

One normally expects some outcome from a discussion. In order for those taking part to have some idea of the outcome it is important to provide an indication of possible action that could be taken.

Conclusion

The conclusion should summarise the reason for the discussion and what it is hoped can be achieved by action stemming from the meeting. This will give purpose to the discussion and make people feel that it is a worthwhile effort to attend and comment.

Informative Reports (See Example IV)

An informative report is written, as its name suggests, primarily to give information. It is intended to increase the reader's knowledge about a specific event or possibly to bring the reader 'up to date'. There is often a significant overlap between explanatory and informative reports. By its very nature an explanatory report is informative. The informative report is more general and is approached somewhat differently. The main sections are:

- title, author and date,
- introduction,
- plan,
- body,
- conclusion.

Introduction

This should state what the report is for, the reason for writing it and what it is hoped will be achieved.

Plan

This part can sometimes be incorporated in the introduction. In informative reports the plan is very important because different readers may be more or less interested in different sections. The information in the report may cover a wide area, but there must always be a reason for including it. The plan clearly shows how each part of the report fits together.

Body of the Report

There are a number of ways the body of the report may be organised. The most effective is to produce a number of sections each of which deals with one main piece of information. Care must be taken to see that each section relates to the others. There must be an overall theme. The aim is to increase the reader's knowledge. This will not be achieved if the reader has to jump from one subject to another.

Conclusion

Normally the conclusion of an informative report should state the reason why the report has been written and what if anything it is hoped will happen next.

Each of these four basic approaches can and should be used with some degree of flexibility. Each report that you have to write will lend itself to one or other of the approaches suggested. You must select the approach which you think is most effective and which allows you to present the information and ideas in the most meaningful way. This can and very often does depend on the content of the report.

Chapter 4
CONTENTS

Collecting and organising the content of a report are vital steps in report writing. However well written a report, it will fail if the basic facts and figures upon which it is founded are incorrect, inadequate or irrelevant.

Every comment, example, reference and suggestion included in a report must be well researched, accurate, meaningful and relevant to the purpose of the report. Asking questions such as 'does it add to the argument?' 'is it new?', 'does it make sense?' may help in eliminating some of the irrelevances. The only way of making sure that the content is worth presenting is by painstaking, tedious and sometimes soul destroying analysis, which leaves no doubt in the reader's mind that the report is based on a thorough study of the problem.

Organising content is a crucial job which should follow the steps listed below.

Definition: Define the purpose of the report and determine which type it is i.e. persuasive, explanatory, discussive or informative.

Analysis: Analyse the subject to determine the main features which will need to be examined.

Collection: Collect the data necessary to study each feature of the subject.

Arrangement: Sort the information.

Examination: Examine the information and draw conclusions, make suggestions as appropriate.

Preparation: Prepare the information for presentation.

Writing: Assemble the information and write the report.

Definition

You must alway start by knowing *why* you are writing the report. Silly as it sounds this is often the most difficult part of the whole process. The dividing line between different types of report

can be fine and only by knowing the purpose can the right
be selected. This selection is crucial to the way in which the
of the report is produced. You may consider that the reasons are
obvious, if you do, check. The obvious reasons are often the wrong
ones.

Analysis

There are very few subjects which can be reported on without
detailed analysis. Very often people are so immersed in their own
subject that they make assumptions which are far from true. They
then call upon their specialist knowledge and experience in support
of their opinions. There is never any harm in checking the validity
of assumptions and studying the subject to separate the important
aspects from the trivial.

Unfortunately reports are written in which the greater part of
the space is devoted to trivial items, giving scant attention to the
really important ones. This can be avoided only by careful analysis
of the subject under the report writer's miscroscope.

Collection

The ability to collect information merits a book of its own. In
the space available here it is only possible to list the key activities
that have to take place:

- decide what information is required,
- discover the sources of the information,
- go to the sources and obtain the information,
- check that the information is accurate,
- check that the information is relevant to the subject.

These five simple sounding steps can in fact take even an experienced
person quite some time to complete. The sources of information
could be people, files, libraries, previous reports, in the computer, in
archives or simply not exist. Access could be open, restricted or
unavailable. The source may be biased, hence the information must
be checked, which is not always possible.

Ambiguity and contradiction must be eliminated by further
questioning, until finally you are happy that the information is:

> accurate,
>
> meaningful,
>
> and relevant.

Arrangement

The information must now be sorted. This is the first point at which the layout of the report is considered. The easiest way is to make a file, which might quite simply be a manilla folder, for each section of the report. The information is then sorted and placed in each of the files. When all the information has been found a home it is reviewed to see whether it is relevant to the section. When this sorting process is complete, consideration can be given to producing the report.

Preparation

The first stage in actually producing the report is the preparation of the material. Information in the form it has been collected, interview notes, extracts from books, sections of other reports, is rarely in the right form for presentation: it must be prepared. This may mean drawing graphs or diagrams, producing tables of figures, re-writing extracts, writing précis and re-wording verbal comments. This stage can often take longer than actually writing the report. However, if this stage is ignored then it is certain that the resulting report will at best be longer than necessary, and at worst completely ineffective.

Writing

The actual process of writing the report will vary from person to person. One of the following methods will be used:

— dictated to a person or machine,

— hand written,

— typed.

Each person must select the method which he prefers. Whichever method is used the report can be written in one of three ways:

— from beginning to end,

— from end to beginning,

— in sections in any order.

Each of these approaches has its merits and the choice depends upon the person and the subject. The inexperienced report writer may find the 'beginning to end' the easiest to manage at first. If the previous stages have all been followed then the writing stage should not pose too much of a problem.

The first draft is read and altered and becomes the second, and hopefully, final draft which is then converted into the final report.

No booklet of this size can possibly deal with all the problems of effective writing.

Some people will always be better writers than others. However, if the stages of preparation as outlined above are followed, then even a moderate writer will produce a good report. Reports, thank goodness, stand or fall on the quality of the content, not on the literary style and finesse of the author.

Chapter 5

FORM

The form a report takes will depend upon three factors:

— the type of report,
— the approach taken,
— the content.

It is not necessary to decide on the form until the first draft is being prepared. It is only at this stage that the way in which the material is to be handled becomes clear. There are three classic formats that can be used:

Logical — Step by step presentation of each part.

Sectional — Dealing with each main feature in its entirety section by section.

Creative — Where the writer deals with the subject in stages leading to a conclusion, but not necessarily in sequence.

Logical

The logical report is written in sequence, taking the reader from a specified starting point (introduction) to a definite end (conclusion) in a series of steps, each of which leads directly from the preceding one. Explanatory and informative reports are most frequently written in this style. (Example II).

The advantages of the logical report stem from the ability to take the reader step by step through the subject, so that by the time the conclusion is reached the report has achieved its aim. Unfortunately such reports become rather tedious to read and, unless written in a brief simple style, confusing in spite of being logical. The reason for confusion arising is in the handling of the content of the report, which can often require a good deal of back-tracking and cross-reference. When this occurs it tends to produce a disjointed format and the reader has to jump backwards and forwards.

Sectional

The sectional report overcomes the problem of the logical report by dealing with each feature of the subject in a separate section.

The sections are drawn into a meaningful whole by the introduction and the conclusion. The advantages for the reader are the opportunity to read each section without the need to refer to other sections and to draw conclusions in stages. The problem with the sectional report is the need to link sections. If attention is not paid to careful preparation it is possible to include irrelevant sections. (Examples III & IV).

Creative

This report is really a combination of the preceding forms. The basis of the creative report is the use of the content to convince the reader and most persuasive reports should be of this type. The creative report takes the form of a written discussion presenting ideas and comments in what appears on the surface to be an illogical sequence. However, when properly written, the creative report can be much more effective than one written in an apparently logical sequence. (Example I).

Guidelines on presentation

The following guidelines on presentation apply equally to the three classic report formats mentioned above:

- Use appendices to remove detail from the body of the report.
- Ensure the report can be read from introduction to conclusion without the *need* to refer to appendices.
- Provide a method of referencing to enable the reader to use the report.
- If the advantages are included make sure the disadvantages are also included.
- Use the minimum of words to make the point.

There is no one form of report which is better than another. Some organisations have established procedures for writing reports. Others leave it entirely to the individual. Unfortunately you only know whether you have chosen the right form when you receive the readers' comments.

Chapter 6
NUMBERING

The way in which reports are numbered always seems to cause people to take strong viewpoints from which it is almost impossible to move them. This is unfortunate because the purpose of numbering reports is to aid the reader, the writer and the printer in the handling of the content.

There are three levels of numbering:

1. the report itself;
2. the sections of a report,
3. the content.

Reports

The way in which a report is numbered will depend to a large extent on the policy within the organisation. If there is a method of allocating a number to each report on a specific subject then it is a useful device. This would however require some form of central control. There is nothing to stop each department operating its own numbering system. Using self-explanatory titles and dates works quite well, but if the cost of administering a numbering system can be justified, it is to be prefered.

Sections

The content of reports should be clearly referenced so that the reader can pick out any part of the report. To do this efficiently means three levels of numbering:

1. sections;
2. appendices;
3. pages.

Sections should be summarised in the introduction and should each be allocated the first level of reference. This may be numerical or alphabetical. Whichever method is used for the main sections the appendices should be the opposite, i.e. if the main sections are numbered the appendices should be alphabetical and vice versa.

Pages should always be numbered sequentially starting with the first page after the title page. The page numbering can be straight through including appendices or separate for the appendices.

Content

The level of numbering within the content depends to a great extent on the detail and the way in which it is organised. It is possible to write a report consisting of main section headings and paragraphs, requiring only two stages of numbering. If, however, sub-paragraphs or lists are introduced then further stages of numbering will be used.

Methods of Numbering

The use of four forms of reference provides considerable scope in numbering reports:

Numbers	—	Arabic
	—	Roman
Letters	—	Capital letters
	—	Small letters

Any combination can be used so long as it aids the reader and is consistent. The numbering method used in the examples in this booklet is as follows,

1	Section headings
1.1	Main paragraphs
1.1.1	Sub-paragraphs
a)	Lists within paragraphs
i	Items within lists
A	Appendices

This form of numbering is mainly decimal but changes at the fourth level to alphabetic and then to roman. The reason for mixing style in this way is to avoid the references becoming awkward to use and to avoid confusion. (Example III).

Any combination of referencing styles can be used provided that it:

— is consistent throughout the report,
— covers every possible reference level,
— does not confuse the reader,
— and, helps the reader to use the report.

Chapter 7
PRODUCTION

The way the report is produced has an important effect on the reader's approach to the report. The guidelines offered here are not exhaustive and professional printers will be able to offer a variety of techniques which should meet the needs of most report writers.

Production can be looked at in several stages as described below:

— Printed content,
— Artwork,
— Re-production,
— Binding,
— Indexing.

Printed Content

The vast majority of business reports will be type written. If modern electric typewriters are used the effect is very good. If a higher quality is required then the content must be type-set, this can be justified (the lines starting and ending at fixed margins) or unjustified (starting at a fixed margin ending at a random point). Type setting is expensive and is rarely warranted.

The type face used will affect the appearance of the report and there are many different styles and sizes of type face than can be used. For type written material the choice is usually between 10 pitch (ten letters to the inch) or 12 pitch (twelve letters to the inch). The letters can be equally spaced or proportional (e.g. W taking up more space than i).

Choosing a type face is important for appearance and readability, though it is recognised that different people have different preferences.

Spacing of the content is very important. There should be adequate margins on the left and right, particularly on the left which is the most likely side for binding. Space must be left between sections and paragraphs so that they stand out. The level of content can be achieved by indenting. Too little on a page is far better than too much.

There are several conventions which should be followed, all of which are based on consistency:

— if possible do not split paragraphs over pages;
— only use underlining for headings;
— words in the text for 1 to 10 and figures above this;
— never start or end a sentence with numbers;
— never mix figures and words e.g. 10 thousand;
— clearly number all charts, diagrams as Figure 1 etc.

These conventions are all intended to improve the readability of the content, but they also prevent typing and type setting errors.

Artwork

If any information is to be presented in a visual form, i.e. graphs, charts, photographs then it should be produced according to the following rules: (Example IV):

— it must be directly relevant to the text and located as close to the point of reference as possible;
— it should be easy to follow and must make the point with impact
— it must be referenced and titled;
— there must be a key;
— as black and white re-production is the most usual make sure the lines, bars etc. are clearly identifiable;
— it must be well prepared by professionals if high quality is required.

If the above rules are followed then artwork can be extremely effective. Unfortunately if the artwork is poor the effect is the exact opposite; it becomes a distraction and will spoil the report.

Re-Production

Increasingly to-day there are two forms of re-production:

— printed,
— photocopied.

Printed reports may be produced on a variety of machines from simple stencil duplicators to letterpress printing. In between there are a number of techniques available. Whichever method is used it is necessary to make a printing stencil or plate. Perhaps the easiest approach is to have the type written report photographed onto a printing plate. This is one of the most widely used techniques for reports and saves the preparation of a special plate.

With the improvement in the quality of 'plain paper' photo-copying machines more and more reports are being produced by directly copying the original typed report. This is an economical and effective method for up to approximately fifty copies which should cover most needs.

With the development of colour photocopying the day of the inexpensive multicolour report is only round the corner.

Whichever method of re-production is used, check the master copy for errors and omissions before the copies are taken. If the report is type set insist upon the preparation and checking of a proof.

Binding

Binding has two values for a report. Firstly it improves the appearance and secondly it protects the contents. There are a variety of binding systems available. The choice of which is the most appropriate will depend upon the following:

— the size of the report (thickness),
— the need for amendments to be made, i.e. fixed or loose leaf,
— the number of copies,
— cost of binding methods,
— distribution requirements,
— quality required,
— the need for special inserts, plans, maps etc.

Binding should always be considered. There are several inexpensive systems available which can be used in any office to considerably increase the quality and appearance of reports.

Indexing

The use of some form of indexing should be examined. If the report has a number of appendices which will be referred to, it is easier if each appendix is labelled and indexed. In reports this can be done in three main ways:

— cut pages.
— overlapping pages,
— side indexing.

Cut pages (see fig. 2) are effective but a nuisance to prepare unless the report is professionally produced and has a wide circulation.

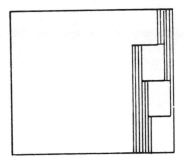

FIG. 2. – CUT PAGES

Overlapping pages are easier to produce than cut pages but are really only effective for thin reports. (see fig. 3).

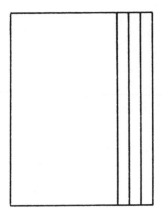

FIG. 3. – OVERLAPPING PAGES

Side indexing is normally done in two ways. The first is the use of an index card which is cut out to leave a small visible section. These are commonly used in ring binders for separating and indexing the content. The other method is to attach a self-adhesive label which protrudes from the edge of the page and produces an effect similar to the card. These two methods are the most commonly used and are both very effective in helping the reader to use the report.

Great care should be taken to see that the effort spent in preparing the report is not lost by lack of thought for the production requirements, which can often make or break the report.

Chapter 8

DISTRIBUTION and FOLLOW UP

Distribution

Reports are normally produced with a particular audience in mind. This audience will become the distribution list.

It is important when sending the report to use a covering letter which explains why the person is receiving a copy. The actual distribution process must ensure that each person receives his copy at the same time.

The covering letter should be headed with the title of the report and then briefly summarise it's purpose. Any time scale for comment or dates of meetings should also be indicated.

The order in which distribution lists are typed often gives rise to problems of status. It is much safer and easier to produce the list in alphabetical order than to try to follow the 'pecking order'.

The following is a typical example. (Example IV).

MEMO

From — T.J. Bentley

To — Mr. C. Apple
     — Mr. D.E. Bruce
     — Mr. J. Greed
     — Mr. P.L.Horton

Date — 3rd July, 1977
     — Mrs. C. Willis

Vehicle Utilisation — Pilot Scheme
Evaluation Report

Please find enclosed a copy of the above report, which I am sending you so that you are fully aware of what is going on. The report evaluates progress to-date and highlights some areas where improvements could be made. Your comments would be appreciated. It is possible that the pilot scheme will be discussed at the next board meeting on the 16th and I would like to be fully aware of your views by then.

Confidentiality is another factor to be considered when distributing the reports. Many companies have established categories which include or exclude certain personnel, others have no such established approach. The safest approach is to ask the person responsible for requesting the report who should receive copies.

Follow up

Having distributed the report it is important to follow it up by contacting each person on the distribution list. This contact might be very brief, just a check that the person has received his copy and, if possible, to gauge his initial reaction. More detailed discussion may follow depending upon the nature of the report.

It is the report writer's responsibility to see that the report achieves its purpose and he must follow it up to see that this happens.

It is practical and often desirable to circulate a draft report to one or two key people to obtain their views on the basis that the report can be altered to include their ideas. This has two beneficial effects. Firstly, the person concerned usually reads the report thoroughly and highlights errors and omissions. Secondly, when the final report is circulated the person is almost honour bound to support it, as he feels that it has already had his approval.

It maybe necessary to write a follow-up report which shows how action stemming from the first report has been introduced and whether or not it is effective. Whenever a follow-up report is written it should carry the same title as the original report, possibly with a sub-title, and should refer to the original report in the introduction.

Chapter 9
CONCLUSION

Report writing is neither an art nor a science. If the guidelines set out in this booklet are followed it will be possible to write effective reports. No one is going to receive a literary award for report writing. The ability to write an effective report may, however, have a significant effect on your career.

A report will be effective if:

— **it is short,**
— **readable,**
— **relevant,**
— **thorough, and**
— **useful.**

FURTHER READING

Complete Plain Words: Sir Ernest Gowers (Penguin 1970).

Effective Presentation : the communication of ideas by words and visual aids : A Jay (Management Publications Limited, 1971)

Information, Communication and the Paperwork Explosion : T J Bentley (McGraw Hill, 1976)

Presenting Reports Effectively : L J Linnet (article; Management Services, Vol. 20, No. 11, 1976)

Report Writing for Management : W J Gallagher (Addison-Wesley, 1969)

Technical Report Writing : H M Weisman (Merrill, 1966).

Writing Reports for management decisions : D M Robinson (Merrill, 1969)

EXAMPLES

EXAMPLE I

Example of a Persuasive Report

This report was written to recommend improvements in procedures for filing and retrieval of information by using microfilm equipment.   Attitudes of the staff and managers involved were mixed, so a good case had to be made.

The report was accepted and implemented according to the recommendations in the report.

The report is based on a report issued in 1974.   Only the company, department names and the dates have been changed.

The report is a good example of a persuasive report (page 12) and is organised in the way suggested in this booklet.   It was not necessary to produce appendices although it would have been possible to produce an appendix for section 5.2 on Savings and Benefits. On balance however, it was felt more effective to leave these in the body of the report.

The style of the report is creative (page 29) moving the reader always towards accepting the benefits until, by the time he reads the section on costs, he is able to justify them.

Example I
Persuasive Report

EFFECTIVE USE

of

MICROFILM

Trevor J Bentley   December 1976

ORGANISATION & METHOD REPORT

Effective use of Microfilm techniques and equipment

1. **Introduction;**

1.1 The use of microfilm techniques is an extremely effective means of reducing clerical costs in the areas of filing and access to information. The principle values of using these techniques are:—

    1.11   Reduction in stationery costs

    1.12   Speed of access to copy

    1.13   Saving of space and handling

    1.14   Improved file security

2. **Summary of Recommendations**

2.1 That the use of microfilming techniques be extended by the purchase of up to date equipment.

2.2 That the films so produced are used as basic reference files, rather than filing originals for immediate reference and films for long term.

2.3 That the equipment be located in the user departments where it can be used on a regular systematic basis.

3. **Present Position**

3.1 At the present time there are two cameras and a reader-printer situated at Head Office. These are used as follows:—

    3.11   Purchase Invoices for three divisions

    3.12   Remittance advices for all divisions

    3.13   Sales Invoices for four divisions

    3.14   Statements for four divisions

    3.15   Conveyance Notes for two divisions

3.2 The films produced form a backup, filed centrally, to the copy files located in the departments concerned.

3.3 In order to provide the films for storage the following procedures are followed:

    3.31   Purchase Invoices:—

        Originals filed in purchase department are removed from the file and filmed and then replaced on file. Files are retained for up to two years, and the films are infrequently referenced.

    3.32   Remittance Advices:—

        Top copy is de-collated, burst and despatched to the supplier. The second copy is filmed in continuous form, then burst and filed.

    3.33   Sales Invoices:—

        Top copy is de-collated, burst and despatched to the customer. The second copy is filmed in continuous form, then filed.

    3.34   Statements:—

        Top copy is de-collated, burst and despatched to the customer. The second copy is filmed in continuous form then burst and filed.

    3.35   Conveyance Notes:—

        When the computer has finished with the tickets they are filmed batch by batch and then sent to the appropriate office.

3.4 The approximate number of documents filmed per annum is as follows:—

Purchase Invoices	150,000	takes	60 rolls film
Remittances	60,000	takes	25 rolls film
Sales Invoices	350,000	takes	140 rolls film
Statements	180,000	takes	72 rolls film
Conveyance Notes	600,000	takes	150 rolls film

3.5 The methods of filing the documents are shown below:—

Purchase Invoices	—Numerically within Month within Depots
Remittances	—Alphabetically

Sales Invoices	—Numerically within Division/Region within Month
Statements	—Alphabetically within Division/Region
Conveyance Notes	—Numerically within Day within Depots.

4. Scope of Survey

4.1 The present use of microfilm, and the continuing use of hard copy files does not appear to offer any benefits, especially as referencing is done principally to the files rather than film. In addition the use of files demands production of copies to fill them, and the associated handling.

4.2 The equipment used at present was examined in the light of up to date equipment, and the most effective means of using microfilm. The costs of existing stationery and films can be considerably reduced by concentration on one or the other, but not both.

5. Observations on Recommendations

5.1 Systems approach to microfilming, depends on the use of the right equipment in the right place at the right time. This approach applied to the following documents can create significant savings.

   5.11   Purchase Invoices:

   To be filmed in Purchase Department using existing camera, with facilities for reading, using existing reader/printer. One month's invoices on file the rest filmed.

   5.12   Remittance Advices:

   Filmed from continuous stationery, processed and filed in Purchase Department, where suppliers queries are checked using existing reader/printer.

   5.13   Sales Invoices:

   Filmed from continuous stationery, processed and sent to Area Sales Offices where customers queries will be checked using new reader/printer.

   5.14   Conveyance Notes:

   Filmed singly in Customer Queries section using new camera, and processed and filed in Customer Queries section. Any queries from customers or depots will be answered by reference to film, using reader/printer.

5.15 Statements:

Filmed from continuous stationery and then despatched to Customer Queries for processing, filing and reference.

5.2 Savings and Benefits

5.21 Savings on computer stationery £2,366 per annum.

Additional cost of films and cassettes less processing savings £ 331

Net annual savings £2,035

5.22 Other less tangible benefits:—
less de-collating
less bursting
less filing
less need for storage space
less paperwork to handle
speed of access to information
ease of distribution

5.3 Equipment costs and location

5.31 Equipment costs:—

Continuous stationery camera	£2,250
Film processor	£2,350
Portable camera	£ 825
Reader printer (2)	£2,850
Reader	£ 179
	£8,454

5.32 The equipment will be located as follows:

Customer Queries	Processor	New
	Camera	New
	Reader/Printer	New

Purchasing Dept.	Reader/Printer	Existing
	Camera	Existing
Computer Dept.	Continuous Stationery	
	Camera	New
Areas Sales Office	Reader/Printer	New
	Camera	Existing
	Reader	New

6. Conclusion

The recommendations in section 2 form the basis for a more efficient service to customers, suppliers and depots, and will considerably improve the existing methods of handling paper-work at Head Office.

EXAMPLE II

EXAMPLE OF AN EXPLANATORY REPORT

Explanatory reports are not easy to write and so there are very few good examples available. The report contained in this example is based on one written some years ago. The names have been changed and the circumstances altered so that the project is no longer recognisable as the original project.

This example of an explanatory report covers all the main points discussed earlier (page 14). The appendices mentioned in the example have been excluded because of space and because they would have added little to the value of the example. Most of the appendices were attached as evidence where it was felt necessary to do this to support comments within the report.

The report has been prepared in a logical style (page 28) taking the reader step by step through the content adding additional facts as each paragraph is read. Numbering is important as on several occasions it is necessary to cross refer to an earlier paragraph.

Following the receipt and discussion of the original report the company concerned re-appraised its cost control procedures and made a number of changes.

Example II

Explanatory Report

COLLINGTON TERMINAL

A report on the reasons for the loss incurred
on the contract

Trevor J Bentley   October 1977

Collington Terminal

1.   **Introduction**

1.1   This report has been prepared to explain the circumstances which led to the completion of the Collington Terminal contract at a loss of £250,000.   The report has been prepared by an investigating team headed by Trevor Bentley, a senior executive with the company and a qualified cost and management accountant.

1.2   The report is intended to provide a complete picture of the events leading up to, during and upon completion of the contract.   To do this effectively the team were given authority to interview any persons they wished and to examine any documents they considered relevant to the subject under scrutiny. This report is the outcome of the team's investigations.

2.   **Persons Involved**

2.1   In order to avoid confusion all persons and departments involved will be referred to by titles.   In certain cases the title has been abbreviated as shown below in brackets:

    Contract Manager

    Chief Estimator

    Area Accountant

    Central Buyer

    Client

    Architect

    Structural Steel and Foundation Contractors (SSC)

    Plant Manager

    Site Foreman

    Site Planning and Control Engineer (SPCE)

    Construction Director

3.   **Sequence of Events**

3.1   The company was first approached by the client in January, 1975.   At this time the idea for a Collington Terminal was a vague one.   The client had not fully considered the problems concerned.   The client commissioned the company to examine the feasibility of such a terminal and to produce initial plans suitable for submission for outline planning permission.

3.2 The sequence of events from this report to the client accepting the company tender were as follows:

Date   Event

1975

Jan. 12   Company employed an Architect to produce a basic proposal.

Feb. 23   Company received the basic proposal.

Mar. 3   Proposal was discussed at board meeting.

Mar. 6   Amendments submitted to architect.

April 18   Architect submitted draft plans.

May 4   Company accepted the draft plans.

June 2   Company produced a project proposal (Appendix A) for the client.

July 16   Client accepted the proposal subject to a number of amendments and requested that the company submit a tender (Appendix B).

Oct. 24   Company submitted a complete tender.

Nov. 19   Client accepted the tender and signed the contract.

3.3 During the above sequence of events full and detailed investigations were carried out on the site by the Company's normal contractors for structural and foundation work. The report from the SSC indicated a need for deep foundations requiring pile driving. This had been allowed for in the contract price.

3.4 On November 25th company appointed a contract manager and a meeting was held to discuss the contract. This was attended by:

                Contract Manager
                Architect
                Chief Estimator
                Area Accountant
                Site Planning and Control Engineer (SPCE)

3.5   The meeting agreed the approach that should be taken to the contract and asked the SPCE to produce detailed plans and schedules of material requirements. The minutes of the meeting are attached as Appendix C.

3.6   On the 4th January 1976 a second meeting was held comprising the same people with the addition of the SSC. At this meeting the contract schedule (Appendix D) was approved.

3.7   On the day following the meeting the client was sent a copy of the schedule with a proposal that work should commence on 1st April, 1976.

3.8   The contract started on the due date and continued without any problems until the 29th August when the monthly progress report was produced (Appendix E). This showed that expenditure on structural steel, concrete and plant hire, all concerned with foundations, was higher than the original plan.

3.9   The contract manager called a meeting on the 4th September attended by:—

> Area Accountant
> SSC
> Architect
> Chief Estimator
> Central Buyer
> SPCE.

3.10 The meeting resolved that due to geological problems the contract would need to be extended by two months and that the client should be approached with a view to obtaining an increased price.

3.11 The contract manager and architect approached the client on 10th September 1976. The extension to the contract was agreed but no further price increase was accepted.

3.12 The project continued until 3rd December 1976 when the site foreman reported a crack in one of the main pillars. The fault was investigated the same day and the contract manager authorised a reinforcement of the foundations.

3.13 The contract proceeded without further problem until the April 1977 progress report was received by the construction director. This showed a significant increase in the cost of structural steel supplies.

3.14 On the 28th April the construction director held a meeting with the contract manager and SSC. At this meeting the causes for the increased costs were discussed and the construction director sanctioned the final supplies required to complete the contract.

3.15 On the 4th May the contract manager was formally repri-manded by the construction director and moved onto a different contract. On the same day the construction director wrote to the SSC indicating that on completion of the contract they would not be working for the company again.

3.16 The contract was completed on the 23rd June.

3.17 The final contract accounts produced on the 11th August indicated a loss of £250,000.

3.18 At the board meeting on 5th September it was decided to carry out an investigation into the Collington Terminal Contract.

3.19 October 12th 1977 this report was presented to the construction director.

4. Action Taken

4.1 There were several key actions which contributed to the loss on the Collington Terminal, these were (Ref. in brackets is the paragraph number of the sequence of events section).

4.1.1	Preparation of project proposal	(3.2)
4.1.2	Structural Steel and foundation contractors report	(3.3)
4.1.3	Submission of the tender	(3.2)
4.1.4	Preparation of the control plan and materials schedule	(3.5)
4.1.6	Meeting on 4th September	(3.9)
4.1.7	Site foreman's report on 3rd December	(3.12)
4.1.8	August 1977 progress report	(3.13)
4.1.9	Meeting on 28th April	(3.14)

4.2   Each of these key factors is analysed below. No conclusions have been drawn by the investigating team. Where the words are those spoken by the person concerned they appear in (   ) otherwise the following comments are reported on the basis of the team's interpretation.

4.3   **Project Proposal** (Appendix A)

This was prepared by the Contract Manager, the Architect and the SSC. It was a broad proposal which gave an indication of the project time scale, an outline of the structural approach, an artists impression of the finished job and a statement of main constraints.

One of the constraints mentioned was the need for special foundations if the terminal was to be built on the client's site.

4.4   **Report of SSC**

The team have been unable to trace any form of written report other than a letter from SSC stating that they would need to have some special pile driving equipment for the contract. Any other information had been given verbally. The chief engineer at SSC had stated quite categorically that he discussed the difficulties of the foundations with the chief estimator and the architect at the time when the tender was being prepared. Though both of these gentlemen recall the meeting, neither of them remembers the specific details and are in one accord that the SSC engineer had stated that (the job would be a piece of cake).

4.5   **Preparation of the Tender** (Appendix B)

The tender was prepared by the Chief estimator. He was given full details of the structural steel, concrete and plant hire from SSC who only quoted for labour. The company was therefore responsible for obtaining prices on these items. The chief estimator stated that due to the pressure to complete the tender he had used the latest prices for steel and concrete given him by the central buyer, and then he (added a contingency allowance of 10% for inflation and quality variations). The plant hire had been arrived at by (inspired guesswork) as it was unusual plant that the company had never used before. These three major items together with site clearance and preparation made up 52% of the contract cost.

4.6 Contract Plan and Material Schedule (Appendix D)

The detailed plan and material schedule was prepared and used as a basis for forward ordering of materials. By reference to the orders it was clear that the price of steel at the time of ordering was 15% higher than that used in the tender. This was either not checked or was overlooked as no one we interviewed had noticed the fact. The planning and control engineer had recognised a discrepancy in the quantities which he pointed out to the contract manager. When they checked it appeared that the figures given by SSC were 20% short of those required. To ensure the quantities agreed with the schedule the contract manager reduced the pile depth by 20%.

4.7 August 1976 Progress Report (Appendix E)

The progress report was prepared by the Area Accountant and showed that more had been spent on structural steel and concrete than was allowed for in the whole contract and 80% of the plant hire allowance had been spent. The work done statement indicated that the main site work was only 70% complete and that a further £80,000 would be needed for further supplies of steel and concrete to complete. The Area accountant had discussed the report with the contract manager and the SPCE.

4.8 Meeting on 4th September

Contrary to general procedure no minutes were kept for this meeting. All those who attended were interviewed and it appears that the main discussion centred on the problems with the foundations. An argument developed between the contract manager and the SSC engineer. This covered the reduction of piling depths which occurred when the material schedules were being examined (4.6).

Each man blamed the other for the fault. It was decided to put the problem right and seek further money from the client. The client refused to pay any more.

4.9 Site Foremans Report.

On 3rd December the site foreman reported (verbally) a crack in a main pillar. The contract manager examined the crack with the SSC engineer, who blamed the contract manager with the comment (if you hadn't reduced the pile depths this would not have happened). The contract manager authorised the strengthening of the foundations which required more materials.

4.10 April Progress Report

The progress report produced in April showed a further increase in material costs, this had not shown up earlier because the invoices had been delayed somewhere in the paperwork chain. Nobody would admit to sitting on the documents. The construction director arranged a meeting for the 28th April, prior to which he had a detailed discussion with the contract manager. In this discussion the construction director made it quite clear that he held the contract manager responsible for the loss. Subsequent to the meeting the contract manager was formally reprimanded and downgraded to the small works department.

5. Cause and Effect

5.1 From the information gathered it would seem that there were three principal causes for the loss on Collington terminal.

These were:—

.1 The price quoted to the client was not adequate to cover all the costs of structural steel, concrete and plant hire.

.2 The lack of a formal report on the foundation requirements which led to the analysis of material requirements being far lower than required.

.3 The change of pile depths in order to reduce the materials caused the crack in the pillar and the extra cost of strengthening.

5.2 These three prime causes led to the over expenditure on the materials concerned, although a subsequent measure carried out by the investigating team indicated a discrepancy in materials used and records of receipts on the site to a value of £40,000. No satisfactory answer has been obtained as to the cause of this discrepancy.

6. Conclusion

6.1 This report highlights the importance of the full examination of site conditions before tendering as well as the need for careful evaluation of tender prices. The disciplinary action of the construction director may have been desirable but the overall supervision of the contract allowed major over-expenditure to occur until it was far too late to correct the problems. It is suggested that the company reviews its contract cost control procedures at the earliest opportunity.

EXAMPLE OF A DISCUSSIVE REPORT

Example III provides an example of a discussive report in the form of a Systems Proposal. The particular example given is based on an actual report, only the company name has been changed.

The report sets out the main points for discussion in the form outlined earlier (page 20). The content of the report is quite specific but leaves room for discussion. No section includes suggestions which could not be amended in the light of the discussion.

The report follows the sectional approach (page 28) although it could be claimed that there is a certain logic in the way it is set out.

It is also a good example of methods of numbering (page 30) showing how different levels of numbering can be used.

The report was fully discussed at a meeting, following which an action plan was agreed and is currently being implemented. The chairman at the meeting issued an agenda comprising each of the main section headings. This ensured that the report was fully discussed and added order and control to the meeting.

Example I
Discussive Repo

SYSTEMS PROPOSAL
FOR
REWARD CONTRACTORS

Trevor J. Bentley

June 1975

1.   Introduction

1.1   This report has been prepared as a basis for discussion on the development of systems in Reward Contractors. In addition to dealing with the specific requirements of Reward Contractors the principles of systems development within the Group as a whole will be outlined.

1.2   The preparation of this report is the result of visits made by systems personnel to all areas of Reward Contractors in addition to two recent visits to North East and Scotland when the principles embodied in the suggestions were discussed with the local managers.

2.   Scope of Systems Requirements

2.1   Reward Contractors existing systems revolve around the accounting control procedures operated at the Regional Offices and at the Head Office. The accounting systems have been designed to ensure accurate financial control and to provide information to management. The systems do provide accurate financial control and do provide a degree of management information. In respect to management information, however, the needs of local management, particularly regarding operating control, are not fully catered for. This is highlighted by the different operating systems and the extraction from local records of other information thought to be of value.

2.2   It is suggested that the existing systems are:—

a)   too slow,

b)   lacking in operational control data,

c)   too financially orientated.

It is not implied that the existing financial control should in any way be reduced but that the detailed level of control should be examined to reduce clerical effort and improve the value of the information produced by the system.

2.3   In short it is suggested that the system should be based on providing management information with financial controls rather than financial control systems with management information.

2.4 The implications of these suggestions for the future systems development is threefold,

    a)   a change of emphasis on the basis of the system framework,

    b)   a change of methods to utilise modern facilities,

    c)   a development towards computerisation to speed up data flow and reduce peak working.

3. Suggested Approach

3.1 Systems development in the Group is based on the following principles:—

    a)   All systems must be designed by management with specialist help and advise.

    b)   Systems must be designed to provide maximum flexibility at the user end, whilst using standard computer-based methods and controls.

    c)   Where computer facilities are required these can be obtained in two ways:—

        i using the Group computer centre,

        ii using outside computer bureaux.

    d)   That systems projects are approved by the management concerned and that the benefits being sought are clearly stated in financial terms.

3.2 Reward Contractors systems framework is indicated below in diagramatic form.

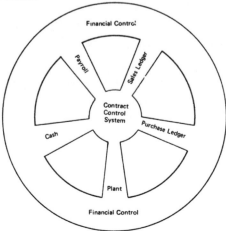

3.3   The operating systems should be the basis of the control systems and should provide a data flow, from which detailed data is used locally for operational control. It is then summarised and cross checked within the system to provide financial control information leading to the production of final accounts.

3.4   There are instances where the benefit of being in the Group and using similar systems can be clearly seen. One particular inter-action is on the buying of materials. It is possible for the supplying Division to provide the following information from the central computer files:—

a)   Up-to-date prices for every material currently being delivered to every Reward Contractors site, separated by cost centre and contract. This would enable the accurate preparation of invoices without delay and allow accurate material costs to be posted to the contract cost records.

b)   Detailed schedule of materials purchased by Reward Contractors, replacing Supplies Division invoices and avoiding to a large extent detailed checking of invoices. (A single invoice could be raised for each Region to cater for VAT).

3.5   Since these points were raised with managers in the North East and Scotland steps have been taken to ensure these facilities can be made available if required. This could be done in a matter of two or three months.

3.6   In order to ensure that management are fully involved with the project it is suggested that a Systems Team is formed comprising the following:—

a)   Group Systems Project Controller

b)   Systems Accountant

c)   An Estimator

d)   A Contract Manager

e)   A Regional Manager

3.7   The project team should be chaired by the Regional Manager and would be a *working* team. Each member would be given specific tasks to perform and would therefore need to give up some time, particularly in the initial design stage   When the agreed System Requirements are handed over to the Systems Development section at HQ for analysis and programming the Systems Accountant could act as the co-ordinator, in addition he should also act as secretary to the team. This method of operation has been found to work very well.

3.8 It will be necessary for the project team to investigate the following areas of activity in detail, and to collect data relevant to the subsequent design of systems:—

    a) Estimating

    b) Contract set up and scheduling

    c) Contract administration and reporting

    d) Contract costing and control

    e) Measuring and invoicing

    f) Sales ledger and credit control

    g) Purchase ledger

    h) Accounting procedures and controls

    i) Management reporting requirements

3.9 Other activities, namely manufacturing will be included and recommendations made on how these activities can be linked into the main systems.

4. Contract Control System

4.1 It is believed that regular information (weekly) for contract monitoring and control is fundamental to improved profits. Though other systems, namely sales ledger, have benefits, it is considered vital that development is based on a contract control system.

4.2 The attached Systems Flowchart (Appendix A) outlines such a system showing the main inputs and outputs. It should be appreciated that this outline is only tentative to show what can be done. Considerable work remains to be done to ensure the design of a practical system.

4.3 The outline includes a weekly contract report which would show the actual costs for the week and the accumulated costs for the life of the contract. It would compare these with the estimated cost of the work done to date. This would be the contract managers main control report.

4.4 The above is only an outline, but it can be seen that the ability of the system to calculate and compare progress in this way is an important step forward in providing management information.

4.5 Cost increase formulae could be incorporated, as could latest material prices, but these sophistications would need to be examined in detail to determine their value.

4.6 The control information would be used in the accounting procedures and the goods received report would provide a basis for checking invoices.

4.7 The system would be used by local management to monitor progress and to determine at an early stage that actual events are deviating from the plan allowed for in the estimate. The information of measures and up-to-date prices should enable more rapid invoicing although it is appreciated that there is no substitute for the on site measure.

4.8 The advantages of the system are:—

    a) rapid information

    b) comparison with estimate for corrective action

    c) the system is based on current practice

    d) reduced effort

    e) virtual elimination of peak working conditions in regional offices

    f) potential cost benefits are considerable e.g. an increase of 1% in actual gross margin is equivalent to £140,000. (The difference between estimated gross margin and actual gross margin is running at between 4% — 8%).

4.9 Disadvantages:—

    a) Improvement in daily reporting techniques could mean some extra work for foremen and supervisors.

    b) Some additional work for estimating in providing the contract file set-up data.

    c) The change of approach which will require new documentation, new equipment and new styles of reports.

4.10 The contract monitoring and control system being the hub of the system wheel will need to be linked to the following systems:—

   a)   Sales Ledger
   b)   Purchase Ledger
   c)   Payroll
   d)   Plant
   e)   Accounts (Nominal Ledger)

These systems may or may not be computer based and so it will be necessary to provide sufficient flexibility to cope with either.

5. Resources

5.1 It is not felt that additional staff will be required in Regional Offices. It is too early to make specific forecasts.

5.2 A systems development team of one analyst and two programmers will be required for approximately one year. This can be one of the existing teams or a new team depending upon the priority and the timing.

5.3 It is believed that computer terminals capable of:—

   a)   data input
   b)   data transmission
   c)   data output, and
   d)   data storage

will be required in each Regional Office and at Head Office.

5.4 It is also considered necessary for these to be able to communicate with the computer centre to either:

   a)   the existing computer, possibly extended to cater for the additional systems, or
   b)   a new mini-computer dedicated solely to this task.

5.5 The anticipated cost of the above requirements is:—

   a)   Systems development team — three men for one year
                                                              £15,000

b)   Terminals at each Regional Office and Head Office (six) at between £4,500 − £6,500 = £27,000 − £39,000

c)   Central facilities   £20,000

d)   Annual maintenance costs for Equipment   £ 5,000

These costs are only estimated, but are within ± 5%.

Offset against this would be the costs of the existing accounting machines and some staff at Head Office, mainly concerned with purchases.

6.   Courses of Action

6.1   The stages in providing the benefits outlined are:−

a)   Approval of this report

b)   Formation of the project team

c)   Initial plan of resources

d)   Formulate the overall programme

e)   Detailed investigation

f)   Preparation of systems requirements   *

g)   Selection of equipment

h)   Ordering of equipment   *

i)   Detailed analysis and programming   *

j)   Testing

k)   Training

l)   Implementation

m)   Review and evaluation   *

* At each of these stages approval will be sought from the Reward Contractors Board before proceeding. A final evaluation will be done to show the degree of success achieved and is normally prepared one year after implementation.

7.   Conclusion

7.1   This report is aimed at obtaining approval to the further investigation into the form of the systems required by Reward Contractors. It is not intended to specify precisely what the system should be, but rather the direction in which we should go to improve the information available to management and thereby increase the overall profitability of the company.

ANAGEMENT SERVICES

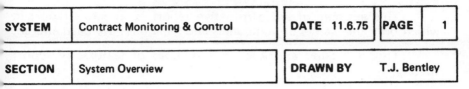

SYSTEMS FLOWCHART

SYSTEM	Contract Monitoring & Control	DATE 11.6.75	PAGE	1
SECTION	System Overview	DRAWN BY	T.J. Bentley	

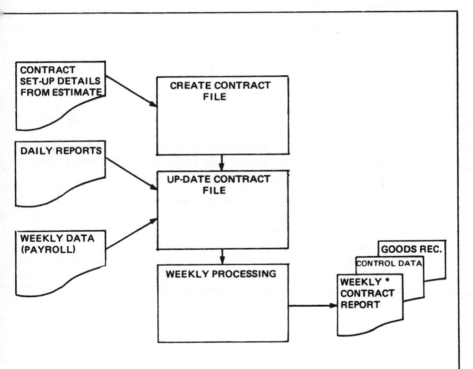

* AN INDICATION OF THE CONTENT OF THIS REPORT IS CONTAINED IN THE BODY
OF THE REPORT

Example IV

EXAMPLE OF AN INFORMATIVE REPORT

This example of an informative report is an actual report in which only the names of companies and locations have been altered.

This is a good example of a number of features of report writing.

These are:

a)   the basic approach to writing an informative report (page 22)

b)   the sectional style of report writing (page 28)

c)   the use of artwork in reports to add impact to the content (page 33)

d)   the method of distribution (see letter on page 37)

You will notice that the report provided an opportunity to make further recommendations (section 2) and also to express thanks to the people concerned (paragraph 8.3).

The appendix attached to the report is a good example of the explanation of the source of data contained in the schedule. To have simply produced the schedule without the explanation would have led to misunderstanding. This proved of considerable value at a later stage when the basis of the comparative figures was questioned by a manager, who was referred back to this explanation by his boss.

Example IV
Informative Report

VEHICLE UTILISATION – PILOT SCHEME
EVALUATION REPORT

O & M DEPARTMENT   July 1977

Vehicle Utilisation — Pilot Scheme

1. Introduction

1.1 The scheme has now been in operation for two full months (May and June). From the introduction of Loadplan in April careful records have been kept of the performance of the company vehicles in the scheme and those company vehicles outside the scheme. This report indicates the results of the analysis of this information, and recommends further action.

2. Recommendations

2.1 That Loadplan continues to be operated in the pilot scheme area as an operational system. (See Sections 4 and 5).

2.2 That Loadplan be introduced into a further group of quarries in the Northern area. (See Section 6).

2.3 That consideration be given to the way distribution is organised in Eastern Area to optimise on the Loadplan system.

3. Analysis of Results

3.1 A detailed schedule is attached, Appendix A, which has been issued as an interim statement of results. From this it can be seen that the earnings per vehicle day have increased throughout the period of operation of Loadplan. This increase is shown in the following charts.

3.2 The average earnings of the company vehicles in the pilot scheme and those outside are shown in Figure 1.

3.3 The earnings of individual vehicles have been recorded and are compared to the average earnings of the whole of the company fleet. This shows in Figure 2 that over the period of the scheme more and more of the vehicles subject to Loadplan have exceeded the fleet average.

3.4 During the pilot scheme, circumstances have varied from depot to depot, as has the understanding and acceptance of the Loadplan system. These points are discussed fully in Section 4 of this report. It is almost certain that the solution of some of these difficulties will lead to further improvement in the performance of vehicles.

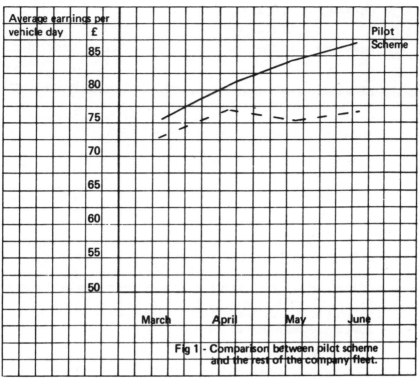

Fig 1 - Comparison between pilot scheme and the rest of the company fleet.

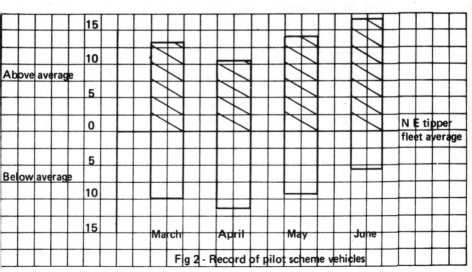

Fig 2 - Record of pilot scheme vehicles

73

4.   Operational Environment

4.1   In any pilot scheme the full importance, advantages and disadvantages, of the basic system only appear under realistic working conditions. Being new, the scheme is the subject of scrutiny and comment from both informed and misinformed personnel who may or may not be directly involved with the day to day working of the system. Loadplan is no exception and has undergone trials in a working environment since April 1977 using 23 vehicles at the following units:—

> Cockby
> Sugar Wharf
> Friarton
> Morton.

Loadplan has been introduced by O & M with the assistance of a full-time Loadplanner regularly visiting each site and co-ordinating vehicle utilisation daily. Telecopiers have been introduced at each unit and at the control centre at Wellington.

Set out below are the salient features of the successful Loadplan implementation at these sites.

4.2   Cockby

Owing to the absence of a permanent full-time weighbridge clerk the scheme has not had a good start.

It would appear that during the trial period orders were satisfied direct from production rather than stock. Production was interrupted on a number of occasions due to plant breakdowns. This caused a reduction in work available for vehicles, which was not always reported to the Loadplanner in time for re-allocation of vehicles to alternative work. The problems were, however, recognised by the Loadplanner during the latter part of the trial period and vehicles were re-allocated. Loadplan highlighted the non-utilisation of vehicles at this site and the actions of the Loadplanner ensured that alternative work was found. Whilst it may be argued that such action might have been taken in the absence of Loadplan, it is considered unlikely.

4.3 Sugar Wharf

During part of the trial period the weighbridge operator was absent due to sickness. This meant that Loadplan training and implementation was not done under the most favourable conditions. Loadplan sheets have had to be completed in retrospect, often by the Loadplanner himself. The telecopier is considered to be a great advantage by weighbridge and production staff in both the dry and coated materials plants. Errors in order information have been eliminated as has the laborious task of taking down information by telephone at inconvenient times.

The Dry Materials plant manager considers that Loadplan has given him greater access to company vehicles because starting and finishing times have improved. He is also of the opinion that the full advantages of Loadplan would be seen if all loads, including hired hauliers, were planned. This is a natural development of the system which would avoid too many vehicles chasing too few loads. This would ease traffic congestion and ensure that the hauliers who remain obtain a full day's work.

4.4 Friarton

The system has been fully accepted by an experienced and knowledgeable weighbridge clerk who organises and monitors his own Loadplan within the system. The telecopier has been of considerable assistance in ensuring that orders are passed in time for vehicles to be loaded for the following day's first drop, and buffer work is available for opportunity loads. In addition there is excellent co-operation between this site and Morton to maximise vehicle utilisation at both locations in the light of changing short-term and unexpected workload requirements.

4.5 Morton

Again the system has been fully accepted by an experienced weighbridge clerk who is regularly operating the Loadplan system with nine company vehicles, most of which are generating high average daily earnings.

The high daily tonnage at this unit and the operation of a large number of company vehicles has maximised the use of the telecopier which is now considered to be vital by the weighbridge clerk to his overall efficiency.

The excellent vehicle utilisation at this unit also reflects to some extent the pre-loading of vehicles for the next day and the availability of buffer work for opportunity loads within the Loadplan framework.

4.6 The Loadplan system has thus been tested under actual working conditions and has stood the test well. In addition it has caused local management, weighbridge, traffic, and distribution staff to examine their actions and to consider the consequences of such actions on the utilisation of transport to the benefit and well being of the company.

5. Changes and Improvements

5.1 A pilot scheme by its very nature tests a basic system under working conditions and results in the proving or otherwise of that system. At the same time areas for improvement arise. The figures presented earlier in this report have, we believe, proved the success of Loadplan. It is felt that the following changes in the system's operation will improve its efficiency.

5.2 The Daily Order Sheet is being re-designed in order to improve the use of the telecopiers.

   a) Provide for the passing of up to 17 (previously ten) orders during one transmission period of six minutes.

   b) Minimise the transmission time required when less than a full sheet of orders is available for transmission, thus making the transmission of even one order cost effective.

   c) Enable the Loadplan to be transmitted with the order sheet thus avoiding the need for another transmission or telephone call.

   d) To facilitate the sending of Dry and Coated orders on one sheet whilst still keeping the types separate for dispatch to different addresses at the receiving site.

5.3 Examination of related systems has highlighted the need for a re-designed delivery ticket (on which information is passed to the Area Sales Office) to assist the weighbridge clerk in his clerical activities.

a) There is a requirement for a "cumulative tonnes" column to enable the weighbridge clerk to check the tonnage delivered at any time without keeping a separate record.

b) The present requirement for separate delivery tickets for each type of material being delivered to the same customer is wasteful of clerical effort at the weigh-bridge.

These problems cannot be overcome immediately owing to effects on the data processing system. However a study is being made with a view to developing a simpler method.

5.3 Staff have been encouraged to comment on the system and this approach will continue with any extension implemented. It has, however, been necessary to make only minor changes and it can thus be safely concluded that the basic concept and system of Loadplan is sound, having withstood the rigours of on-site testing.

6. Extension of Loadplan

6.1 There are two reasons for recommending an extension of Loadplan:—

a) Improvement in the utilisation of the additional vehicles.

b) Improvement in the co-ordination and use of vehicles moving between Eastern and Northern Areas.

6.2 It is suggested that the following units are included in the Loadplan scheme:—

	Vehicles
Newtown	1
Westley	5
Drayton	3
Oakmouth	3
Washington	7
	19

6.3   The annual cost of extending Loadplan is as follows:—

Maintaining existing system		£
Loadplan Officer		4,200
Car		1,600
* Telecopiers 4 @ £300 pa		1,200
1 @ £420 pa		420
Stationery		100
	A	7,520

Extending the system		£
Loadplan clerk		3,200
* Additional telecopiers		
4 @ £300 pa		1,200
Stationery		100
	B	4,500
Plus O & M Charge	C	4,000
A + B + C		16,020

* Three year lease.

6.4   If an improvement of £10 earnings per vehicle day (that is £2,000 per vehicle year) can be achieved, the annual benefits of Loadplan would be:—

a)   Existing scheme   £46,000
b)   Extended scheme   £38,000

7.   Distribution

7.1   With the use of Loadplan, distribution of the company's products can be co-ordinated to ensure that:—

a)   Orders are placed on the most economic supplying unit.

b)   Materials are available.

c)   Vehicles are available.

7.2   In addition changes during the working day can be co-ordinated via the Loadplan officer so that vehicles are not moved to less remunerative work.

7.3   The extension of Loadplan into Northern creates a need to examine the shipping operations and the demand pattern at each unit. This work must be carried out prior to extending the system.

7.4   Close co-operation is necessary between the order office, Loadplan office and the traffic manager. Because of this it is suggested that the Loadplan office is permanently located at Wellington close to the order office. The link between the traffic manager and loadplan officer should be by telephone.

7.5   The report on the implications of Loadplan on the units in the extended scheme will be prepared in advance of the training and implementation of the system.

8.   Conclusion

8.1   If the recommendations of this report are accepted it is · suggested that the following action is taken:—

    a)   Improvements in existing pilot scheme.

    b)   Change existing scheme to a permanent operation.

    c)   Investigate the extension in Northern.

    d)   Introduce Loadplan into Northern area.

8.2   The possible timing for this extension is indicated in Figure 3 below:—

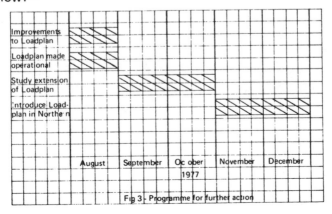

Fig 3 - Programme for further action

8.3   Finally, this is an excellent opportunity to express our thanks
       to all personnel in North East Area who have co-operated so
       willingly in the introduction and operation of Loadplan. Any
       benefits created by the system must be due to their efforts in
       ensuring that the difficulties of changing from one system to
       another were so easily overcome.

LOADPLAN

Interim Statement of Results

1. Introduction

1.1 These notes explain briefly the source of the information shown on the attached schedule. This interim report has been prepared for two reasons.

    a) To show the form in which the information on results is to be presented.

    b) To indicate progress after the initial introduction of Loadplan.

2. Information

2.1 Information has been provided for March, April and May 1977. Though figures were collected for February it is felt that they were untypical and would have shown an unrealistic improvement not associated with Loadplan.

2.2 Work days: These are the normal working days available including ½ day for Saturday when worked, which is on most weeks.

2.3 Vehicles days available:

    These are the days and ½ days that vehicles were available for work.

    In order to make March and April comparable the drivers' work sheets were analysed in detail.

2.4 Earnings: Total earnings are extracted from the computer analysis. The earnings are then divided by the vehicle days available to give the average per vehicle day.

2.5   Rest of Fleet Earnings:

This is the average per vehicle day arrived at by dividing the total earnings (from computer analysis) by the available days (calculated as the same % as the pilot scheme).

The work involved in analysing the work sheets for three months for the rest of the fleet was not considered necessary, as taking the same '% lost time' on the pilot scheme was felt to be satisfactory.

2.6   Company Tonnes Carried:

Total tonnes carried by the vehicles in the pilot scheme. (Computer Analysis).

2.7   Total Tonnes Delivered:

From Marketing Services for the quarries in the Pilot scheme.

2.8   Company % Carried:

Company tonnes carried as a % of the tonnes delivered.

3.   Conclusions

3.1   No definite conclusions can be drawn from the schedule attached, but I believe that the figures indicate that Loadplan is having a direct effect on the performance of the vehicles in the pilot scheme.

3.2   Loadplan was approximately 50% operative in April and 100% operative in May.

3.3   It is anticipated that the figures for June will show a further improvement, though the holiday period, and staff sickness and holiday, will have to be accounted for in producing the comparative figures.

   NOTE: The figures for June have been added to the statement of results.

LOAD PLAN – STATEMENT OF RESULTS

Vehicles in Pilot Scheme	23

DEPOTS IN PILOT SCHEME
COCHBY
MORTON
FRIARTON
SUGAR WHARF

Month	Work Days	Vehicle Days Available	Earnings			Rest of Fleet Average Earnings Per Vehicle Day	Company Tonnes Carried		Total Tonnes Delivered		
			Total	Average Per V. Day	% Inc.		Total	Average Per V. Day	Total	Average Per V. Day	Company % Carr.
			£	£		£					
MARCH	25	537	40463	75.35		72.78	42026	78.26	100891	187.88	41.7
APRIL	20	430	34677	80.64	7.02	76.98	34664	80.61	79924	185.87	43.4
MAY	24	488	41240	84.51	3.87	74.78	39009	79.94	100024	204.97	39.0
JUNE	21½	438½	38177	87.06	3.02	76.88	37618	85.79	93099	212.31	40.4
JULY											

INDEX

appendices 18
approach
    basic rules 14-15
    flexibility of 23
    specific rules 15
artwork 33
audience 10-11
    distribution to 37

binding 34

cause and effect 20, 57
communication, reporting as a means of
    9, 14
confidentiality 38
content 11
    organizing content
        analysis 24, 25
        arrangement 24, 26
        collection 24, 25
        definition 24
        examination 24
        numbering, levels of 31
        preparation 24, 26
        printed 32
        writing 24, 26
creative form 29

definitions 10, 24
discussive reports 13, 20-2
    conclusion 22
    discussion points 21
    example of 59-69
    lack of purpose in 20
    possible action 21
    scope of subject 21, 61-2
distribution 37-8
    audience in mind 37

equipment costs and locations 47-8
examples 42-8, 49-58, 59-69, 70-84
explanatory reports 13, 18-20
    actions taken 19-20, 54-7
    cause and effect 20, 57
    conclusion 20, 58
    example of 49-58
    persons involved 19, 51
    sequence of events 19, 51-4
    things to avoid 19

flexibility of approach 23
flow chart 69
follow up 38
form
    creative 29
    logical 28
    sectional 28-9
indexing 34
informative reports 13, 22-3
    body of report 22
    conclusion 23
    example of 70-84
    plan 22
introduction 16, 44

jargon
    definition 10
    rules about 15

layout
    guidelines 16
    (see examples)
logical form 28

method 11

numbering
    levels of 30
        content 31
        reports 30
        sections 30
    methods of 31

objective of report writing 9-10, 11, 12, 39
organization of material 24-7

persons involved 19, 51
persuasive reports 12, 16-18
    appendices 18
    equipment costs and location 47-8
    example of 42-8
    introduction 16, 44
    present position 17, 44-5
    recommendation, use of 16, 17, 44, 46-7
    savings and benefits 47
    survey, scope of 17, 46
plan 22
present position 17, 44-5

presentation 29
printed content 32
production
    stages of 32, 33, 34, 35, 36
reasons for writing reports 12
    discussive reports 13
    explanatory reports 13
    informative reports 13
    persuasive reports 12
recommendations in reports 16, 17, 44,
    46-7
reporting as a means of communication 9,
    14
reports
    discussive 13, 20-2, 59-69
    explanatory 13, 18-20, 49-58
    informative 13, 22-3, 70-84
    persuasive 12, 16-18, 42-8
report writing
    approach 14-15
    audience 10

content 11, 24-7, 31, 32
distribution 37-8
form 28-9
method 11
numbering 30-1
objective 9-10, 11, 12, 39
production 32-6
writing 24, 26
reproduction 33
rules
    basic 14-15
    specific 15

savings and benefits 47
scope of subject 21, 61-2
scope of survey 17, 46
sectional form 28-9
sequence of events 19, 51, 53
specific rules 15
subject, scope of 21, 61-2
survey, scope of 17, 46